TRIVIA
ON
TAP

TRIVIA
ON
TAP

The Complete Guide to
Bar-Room Banality

LAGOON BOOKS, LONDON

TRIVIA
ON
TAP

Compiled and edited by Hannah Robson
and Nick Hoare
Cover design and 1950's cartoons
by Gary Sherwood
Design and cover label by Linley Clode
Series editors: Simon Melhuish and Emma Craven

Published by
LAGOON BOOKS
PO BOX 311, KT2 5QW, UK

ISBN 189971 221 6
© 1996 LAGOON BOOKS.
Lagoon Books is a trade mark of Lagoon Trading
Company Limited. All rights reserved.

TRIVIA
ON
TAP

The Complete Guide to
Bar-Room Banality

LAGOON BOOKS, LONDON

TRIVIA
ON
TAP

Also available in this series:

Laughs on Draught: The Essential Pub Joke Book
ISBN: 189971 222 4

Lateral Drinking Puzzles: A Cocktail of Conundrums
for Connoisseurs
ISBN: 189971 220 8

The trivia questions in this book are written for your entertainment. The pictures illustrate the questions and not necessarily the answers.

The answers can be found on pages 86 – 90.

Cheers!

TRIVIA
ON
TAP

1

George Melly
described "a sherry at noon, a glass
of wine at lunch, two or three gins, half a
bottle of wine and a couple of brandies
in the evening"
as practically...

...*what?*

In 1959 Ermal Cleon Fraze invented something for which drinkers will be eternally grateful. What was it?

a) *The bendy straw*

b) *Alka-Seltzer*

c) *The ring-pull*

In America in 1790, an **"Anti Fogmatic"** was an alcoholic drink supposed to counteract the bad effects of fog.

True or false?

W.C. Fields said,
'A woman drove me to drink...

a) *which was fair, after all, I'd driven her to distraction.'*
b) *and I never even had the courtesy to thank her.'*
c) *and I thought she hated me.'*

In 1917 why was a workman in Liverpool given three months hard labour for treating his friend to a drink?

TRIVIA
ON
TAP

5

Toulouse-Lautrec's favourite

drink was of his own invention,

called 'Tremblement',

a mixture of the dregs from

all the bottles left

after an evening's drinking.

True or false?

Samichlaus is a Swiss beer whose name translates as Santa Claus. This Christmas tipple is brewed on St Nicholas Day every year – December 6th, and released on the same day exactly one year later.

It also has the acclaim as being the world's strongest beer. If Newcastle Brown Ale is **4.7%** ABV (Alcohol by Volume) and Guinness is **4.3%** ABV, what strength is Samichlaus?

a) *11%*

b) *14%*

c) *19%*

What is the base ingredient in the following liqueurs?

a) *Cynar (Italy)*
b) *St Hallvard (Poland)*
c) *Erdbeergeist (Germany)*
d) *Geburgs Polingen (Germany)*

And the base flavour of the following drinks?

a) *Creme de Pecco (Holland)*
b) *Pasha (Turkey)*

TRIVIA
ON
TAP

8

In 1664 during dinner at

The Clothworker's Company,

a guest at the table, Alderman Cooper,

was overcome by a fit of apoplexy.

In an attempt to revive him, his hosts

dosed him with brandy, whereupon he

died. The next day a mournful Lady

Cooper called on the clerk of the

Company and claimed that she would not

be in her present state of widowhood if...

a) *her husband had been given a cocktail of vinegar, mineral water, mercury and thyme.*

b) *he had been dosed with his usual remedy of Hollands gin.*

c) *her husband had followed her example of taking three quarters of a pint of brandy with his breakfast every morning.*

Cockney rhyming slang has given the English language a variety of euphemisms and metaphors to describe booze and boozing.

a) *Why does the word 'tiddly' mean 'slightly drunk'?*

b) *What are 'elephants'?*

c) *What does 'on the river' mean?*

You may think drink prices in nightclubs and hotels are expensive, but they are nothing compared to these record-breaking tariffs! In 1992 the first glass of Beaujolais Nouveau was auctioned for £982, and in the same year a 1919 Springbank whisky was sold at Fortnums for £6750! But who owned the world's most expensive bottle of wine at £105,000?

Thomas Jefferson, Henry Ford or *Elvis?*

If you were to order poteen in Ireland, what would you get?

a) *A bar room snack*

b) *An illicitly-produced Irish spirit*

c) *A glass of water*

Can you remember which beer is advertised with the following slogans:

a) *'It's what your right arm's for'*

b) *'It looks good, it tastes good, and by golly it does you good!'*

c) *'Stay sharp to the bottom of the glass'*

In Hanover in July 1993
a beer tanker overturned, flooding
the street with thousands of gallons
of beer. The road became blocked
as hundreds of drivers left their
vehicles and filled any receptacle
they could get their hands
on with beer. The impromptu
street party continued for
hours until rain stopped play!

True or false?

TRIVIA
ON
TAP

13

Which of the following
was a nineteenth century
cure for drunkenness?

a) *drinking a distilled liquid extracted from acorns.*

b) *drinking owls eggs which have been cracked into a cup.*

c) *placing a live eel in the drinker's full cup.*

In the 1980's a craze for acronyms swept the country; YUPPY for 'young urban professional'; DINKY for 'dual income no kids yet'.

What does DUMBO stand for?

a) *Drunken upper middle-class businessman over the limit*

b) *Drunk & upset middle-aged boring oldster*

c) *Drunken upwardly mobile banking oik*

In Australia strict licensing laws were brought in by the government as a measure of sobriety during the Second World War, enforcing bars to stop serving at 6 pm. Ironically breweries and pub owners supported the law until the 1950's because they discovered that sales weren't affected so overheads could be kept low. What was the name given to the quick quaffing as Australian drinkers desperately downed their drinks before last orders?

a) *Rummies' Rush*

b) *The Sundown Run-down*

c) *The Six O'Clock Swill*

At ancient Greek feasts, the wine was traditionally cut with salted water to a proportion of **3** parts water to **2** parts wine, and drinkers wore wreaths to protect themselves from noxious fumes.

True or false?

In 1694, Admiral Edward Russell, commander of the British Mediterranean Fleet, entertained 6000 guests at an enormous party. Apart from its size, what was so unique about the party punch?

a) It was served by waiters floating in the garden fountain which had been transformed into a giant punch bowl. The fumes were so intoxicating that the waiters had to work in strict rotation.

b) It contained whole peaches, the stones of which contain cyanogen. This reacted with the other ingredients to produce the toxin cyanide, killing 72 guests.

c) At the end of the party, when the punch had been drunk dry, the Admiral's wife was distraught to learn that her pet poodle was found dead and drowned at the bottom of the largest punch cask.

ON

TAP

18

Imbibriosity means
habitual drunkenness.

True or false?

TRIVIA
ON
TAP

19

In the October Mop
Fair in Dalton-in-Furness
Cumbria, ale tasters were elected
from the local men and given
the glorious task of visiting all the
local pubs to drink their beer!
The best beer was awarded a red ribbon.
How was the worst beer recognised?

   a) *It was shared out among the local*
      women to be used as shampoo.
   b) *It was poured over the offending*
      brewer's head.
   c) *It was used to sprinkle on chips.*

TRIVIA
ON
TAP

20

Which monarch was reputed to drink a quart of ale every morning for breakfast?

    a) King Henry VIII
    b) King John
    c) Queen Elizabeth I

In American slang, what is a 'Dead Marine'?

a) Anyone fast asleep after a heavy drinking session

b) An empty bottle or glass

c) Another term for 'brewers droop'

At one time the word 'boy!' was a common way to order champagne. Why?

a) 'boy!' was a corruption of the French for "bottle". Our aristocratic ancestors' command of French was far from brilliant, and they managed to twist "bouteille" into "boy!"

b) Whilst enjoying shooting parties, King Edward VII was accompanied by a page who would be summoned to refill the king's empty glass of champagne with the command 'boy!'

c) Because it was said that, in polite society, champagne was as essential as a servant boy.

Κing George IV married his cousin Caroline of Brunswick on the condition that Parliament pay off his debts. From such an inauspicious start the marriage was somewhat doomed to failure; Caroline spent many of her married years living in Italy, she was involved in a **'delicate investigation'** into an alleged illegitimate child, and rather than attend the coronation of her husband, she spent the evening at the theatre! What event marked their wedding?

a) George was so drunk that he had to be supported at the altar by his best man.

b) Caroline was more drunk than her husband, delaying the ceremony for 4 hours while she 'returned to herself'.

c) An inebriated George mistook his future mother-in-law for his future wife.

TRIVIA
★ ON ★
TAP

23

Why did some

nineteenth century publicans

put collection boxes

for temperance societies

in their bars?

Where does the expression **'to go on a bender'** come from?

a) It evolves from the slang 'bend' meaning 'to bend one's elbow'.

b) "The Bender" was an early rollercoaster at Coney Island NYC, mentioned in F. Scott Fitzgerald's "The Beautiful & Damned".

c) A "bender" was the name given to the brass bar running along the edge of the bar top. In the 1920's it became synonymous with the fun to be had whilst leaning on it.

A 'dew drink' is a drink made with rainwater.

True or false?

C ritic and wit Dorothy Parker said

'One more drink and I'll be under...

a) the table.'

b) the national average.'

c) the host.'

TRIVIA

ON

TAP

26

Dom Perignon was named
after a blind Benedictine monk who
invented the first sparkling champagne.

True or false?

In which play did

Shakespeare write that drink

"provokes the desire
but it takes away
the performance"?

How did King Charles II of Navarre meet his death?

a) Following doctor's recommendations, Charles the Bad was nightly sewn into a muslin shroud which had been doused in alcohol. One evening, as the page finished his cross stitch, he used a candle flame rather than a knife to break the remaining thread, but the flame simply burnt up into the cloth, ignited the alcohol, and flambéd the king to death.

b) Following a family row, he challenged his son and daughter to a cognac-drinking challenge, which resulted in his death and his son's blindness. His daughter seems to have made a full recovery. Who actually won is not recorded.

c) In an attempt to repair relations with his subjects, he organised a massive three-day midsummer banquet, providing free food and drink. On the first night, the "guests" rapidly became an enraged drunken mob, hanging the King from his gatehouse and burning his castle to the ground.

1 oz of lemon oil,

1/2 oz of lime oil,

3 oz of vodka and

3 oz of red wine

The above cocktail can be applied
externally as a massage treatment for
which of the following conditions?

a) *impotence*

b) *cellulite*

c) *dandruff*

What is potophobia?

a) *Fear of drinks*

b) *Fear of water*

c) *Fear of pubs*

TRIVIA ON **TAP**

31

W hose autobiography
is called **'The Good, The Bad
and The Bubbly'**?

a) *Dean Martin*
b) *George Best*
c) *Oliver Reed*

W hilst drinking port,
if someone asks if you
'know the Bishop of Norwich',
how should you respond?

What would one add to Irish stout to produce the following drinks?

a) *Black Velvet*

b) *Black and Tan*

c) *Brown Velvet*

d) *Black Russian*

If you were to walk into a pub in

early nineteenth century England,

and found yourself jumped upon

by the other punters, your shoes

nailed to the floor, your work tools

hidden, and were forced to lay down

onto a teeth-up coal rake,

what would have been your crime?

Frankinmas falls on the 19th-21st of May, and is a period in which apple blossom is often damaged by a late frost, thus ruining the crop and jeopardising the season's cider. What is the legend surrounding this time?

a) *St Francis is said to have been distraught by the effect of fermented apples on woodland animals. He prayed for a remedy, and ever since, the late frost has been attributed to his intercession on behalf of the squiffy squirrels.*

b) *The applegrowers of medieval Kent would blame the loss of their crop on the French, and would hang effigies of them in the orchards at this time, burning them to ward off the frost.*

c) *Legend has it that Frankin was a brewer of ale who sold his soul to the devil in return for a three day frost which would destroy the rival cider industry. Traditionally the cider makers are thought to have exacted their revenge by spreading a rumour that the pact was completed on the condition that the brewer weaken his ale with water.*

The euphemism 'one over the eight' for drunkenness comes from the days when it was thought that the average man could drink eight pints before becoming legless!

This was before the days when health experts gave recommended limits to daily consumption of alcohol.

In 1979 the Royal College of Psychiatrists suggested an average daily intake of

how many pints?

In 1827 London witnessed the Isle of Dogs Mutiny, during which the crew of the frigate HMS Intrepid took over both their own ship and a merchant barge carrying rum from the Caribbean, and barricaded themselves into the docks. After a ten day siege, the army stormed the gates, to find a very sorry sight – nine men had drunk themselves to death, and the remaining were arrested. Seven men were executed for mutiny.

True or false?

Which of the following
was a common hangover cure
from ancient Egypt?

a) *To rub papyrus oil on the skin at the back of the knees.*

b) *To rest a cabbage on the forehead.*

c) *To drink an infusion of lime juice and vinegar.*

"*To have a sniff of the barman's apron*"
means you have the
propensity to consume a
large amount of
alcohol before becoming drunk.

True or False?

Where in the world is
beer the most widely available
manufactured product in the country?

a) *Kenya*

b) *Equador*

c) *Liberia*

TRIVIA
ON
TAP

39

In the medieval period,

as beer went sour in

hot European summers,

the Swiss blamed the

disaster on 'beer witches'.

To overcome the problem

fifteenth century brewers in

Germany began to

store and brew the beer

at cool temperatures,

often in caves packed with ice.

*What was the name given to
the new cold-fermented beer?*

At a grand dinner, a
disgruntled lady lent toward
Sir Winston Churchill and hissed,
"Mr Churchill, you are drunk". To which
the illustrious statesman replied...

a) *And you, Madam, are ugly. But I shall
be sober tomorrow.*

b) *But not, sadly, as drunk as I should
be given present company.*

c) *If you think I am drunk now, you
should wait until the dessert is served.*

What drink in nineenth century England
was described by the following synonyms:

Cuckold's Comfort
Last Shift
The Gripe
Tom Roe
Lady's Delight?

The Royal Navy

has generously bestowed

on the English language a

number of idioms and euphemisms

for drink and drinking.

Do you know where the following

expressions come from?

a) *'To splice the mainbrace'*
b) *'Grog'*
c) *'Three sheets to the wind'*

In 1858, a famous writer was sent by the Post Office to the West Indies to analyse the local postal service. He commenced his investigation with a very uncomfortable horse ride, but determined not to be distracted, he comforted his chafed posterior in a basin filled with brandy. Who was the owner of the brandy bottom of Barbados?

Austrian troops in World War One discovered that bottles of Tyrolean schnapps would explode on impact if cordite was added to them. A company holed up in a monastery stumbled across this after using the gunpowder in their bullets to remove the fusel oil in the spirit. The combination was never used in battle, due to its instability, but it was used to deter enemy engineers who were attempting to scale the cliffs to the monastery.

True or false?

Who said '*Gin and Water is the source of all my inspiration*' and '*Man, being reasonable, must get drunk; The best of life is but intoxication.*'?

a) *Lord Byron*
b) *Dennis Thatcher*
c) *Keith Chegwin*

TRIVIA
ON
TAP
44

The expression 'toasting' derives from the piece of spiced and toasted bread which was commonly found in British drinks.

True or false?

Here's something you might not want to try at home! In his 'Remaines of Gentilisme and Judaisme' (1881), Aubrey describes a cocktail ingredient which one wouldn't normally expect to find behind the bar, but which, he alleges, has remarkably intoxicating results when mixed with ale.

What was it?

a) Warm goat's urine.
b) Blood from a stud bull.
c) The ashes of burnt human bones.

Charlemagne, King of the Franks and Holy Roman Emperor (742-814), lent his name to the vintage white wine Corton-Charlemagne. Why did the wine come to bear the regal name?

a) *The king was saved during battle on the land where the vineyard now stands. Tradition has it that as he kneeled to thank God for his salvation, he wept with gratitude, and as the tear dropped onto the earth, a vine sprang forth from which the fine white wine is pressed.*

b) *According to legend the king was so fond of the wine that whilst travelling with his court he insisted they detour via the chateau that produced the wine. Following a very drunken evening the king rose early the next day, entered the vineyard, and knighted the vine in his name.*

c) *The white vine was planted on the instructions of his wife, who was tired of seeing the red stain of claret wine on his white beard.*

Warninks, makers of advocaat, have an egg-breaking department with machines which separate the yolks and whites of how many eggs per hour?

a) 900

b) 2,000

c) 18,000

From where does the habit of putting lime in beer originate?

a) *The habit goes back to the 1950's when a Mexican brewery launched a beer which was served in the manner of the traditional drink of Tequila - with salt and lemon.*

b) *It is a pure marketing invention.*

c) *It keeps the flies away from the bottle neck.*

Dr Johnson wrote:

"Claret is the liquor for boys;

port is for men; but he who aspires

to be a hero ... must drink ..."

What?

What is a 'swoon bottle'?

a) A Melbourne bottle-blowing competition, forming a central part of the Yarra River Beer Festival.

b) The bottle Vikings would drink from before going into battle.

c) A small bottle of brandy carried by Victorian ladies in case of emergency.

Where does the expression 'hair of the dog' come from?

a) Thirteenth century doctors would treat the poisoning caused by beer made with impure water by rubbing the stomach of the victim with a dog's pelt soaked in sour beer.

b) The sixteenth century belief that if one has been bitten by a dog, the best antidote to rabies is to apply to the wound the burnt hairs of the dog in question.

c) The werewolf myth; otherwise known as 'once a drinker, always a drinker.'

Which of the following events really takes place in Darwin, Australia?

a) 'Mr Tinnie-verse', in which the competitors prove their drinking virtuosity by drinking beer by the bath-full.

b) 'Beef in Beer Bake-Off', in which the world's largest beef pie is made at the annual Darwin City Festival, the ingredients including 60 gallons of beer.

c) 'The Beer Can Regatta', a boating race for boats made solely from beer cans.

TRIVIA ON TAP

52

Who said

"I am dying beyond my means"

as he sipped champagne in a hotel in Paris before his death?

a) *Jim Morrison (The Doors)*
b) *Oscar Wilde*
c) *Baudelaire*

Who wrote the greatest song title of all time – **I'd rather have a bottle in front of me (than a frontal lobotomy)?**

a) *Randy Hanzlick*
b) *Randy Socksniff*
c) *Randy Van Drijver*

Your good health, Sir!

Where does the expression 'to hob nob' come from?

a) It comes from the Old English 'hab and nab', meaning to give and take, and was originally used to describe the action of toasting.

b) It is derived from Hobnob, a Gaelic goblin who was said to plague drunkards by inciting them to reveal their secrets through drunken chatter.

c) In the eighteenth century British navy, the galley was the only place sailors could chat and drink rum, so they would gather and talk, by the hob. This was punishable by flogging.

TRIVIA
★ ON ★
TAP

54

Which American President was killed whilst his coachman, bodyguard and valet were boozing?

In 1986 Al Capone's secret vault beneath the Lexington Hotel in Chicago was opened live on American TV. The event was accompanied by the usual media circus, and attended by members of the treasury, IRS and CIA, who were all interested in what they hoped to find inside, from money, to the bones of his enemies! So what did they discover when they finally blasted through the walls?

a) *Shares in one of the world's largest rum distilleries.*

b) *Two empty bottles of gin.*

c) *The corpse of Di Angelo Capriccios, pickled in a vat of whisky.*

During the reign of Catherine I of Russia the state ballrooms were filled with women dressed as men, because women were banned from drinking.

True or false?

TRIVIA

ON

TAP

57

On your travels

around the UK,

where would you find

the home of 'the Dog?'

Bob Todd, Benny Hill's bald sidekick, appeared in the first beer commercial ever televised, combing his then-healthy locks before sipping a pint of Courage, scoring treble top in a darts game and asking the blushing barmaid to "come to the pictures tomorrow night".

True or false?

What happens to goldfish immersed in 3.1% of alcohol?

a) *they overturn in 6 – 8 minutes.*

b) *they lose the use of their right fin, thus swimming in tight circles.*

c) *their swim bladders rupture and their gills dilate, causing them to drown.*

What is the traditional drink of Royal Navy Officers?

a) Dark Rum

b) Pink Gin

c) Tia Maria

What spirit is made from the agave plant, which is part of the lily family, has blue leaves and looks like a giant pineapple?

What is balderdash?

a) *The residue left after the repeated pressings in cider making.*

b) *Rustic beer, made from stale bread and rye in medieval England.*

c) *Any adulterated wine or mixed drink.*

Who said...

"We are fighting Germany, Austria and Drink and, as far as I can see, the greatest of these foes is Drink"?

Plonk it down on the table, Missus!

W here does the word 'plonk' come from?

a) Part of the "Plonk it down on the table" catchprase used by "Cheeky" Charlie Church in the 1930's radio show "Please, Mrs Davis".

b) A seventeenth century misinterpretation of "Poulenc".

c) Rhyming slang 'plink-plonk' for vin blanc, made up by British soldiers in the Somme during the First World War.

Brendan Behan wrote

'I only take a drink on two occasions;...

a) when I'm thirsty and when I'm not.'

b) now and then.'

c) when I'm drunk and when I'm sober.'

King Edward IV had

an ongoing rivalry with his ambitious

brother George Duke of Clarence.

The feud was made public by

Clarence who refused to eat or drink

at court so as to stress his

precarious position. He was right to be

afraid, but even if his brother had asked

him *'what's your poison?'*,

he could hardly have expected to

meet his maker as he did.

How did Edward IV

kill his brother?

In ancient Egypt, stonemasons working on the pyramids were paid with a beer which went by the name of Kash. This is the etymological root of the word for money: cash.

True or false?

PONTET CANET
→1887←
BARTON & GUESTIER
BORDEAUX
FRANCE

Which of the following is not a real wine?

Grk,

Lump,

El Lager,

Mascara,

Les Blotters

or

Brown Bastard

A Polish Bison is a mixture of vodka and what?

a) *Shredded peppersteak*

b) *Angostura bitters and Worcester sauce*

c) *Bovril*

W hich book, later made into a film, needed to be written

"in a state of near drunkeness in order to deal with material that upset me so much?"

a) *Forrest Gump*

b) *Under the Volcano*

c) *Clockwork Orange*

TRIVIA

ON

TAP

68

Rhubarb Thrasing is a traditional pub game in which two contestants, sporting blindfolds and earplugs, each stand in a dustbin, and holding on to one another with their left hands, they attempt to beat the other into submission with sticks of rhubarb held in their right hands.

True or false?

About which beautiful film star did Kenneth Tynan say *"What, when drunk, one sees in other women, one sees in .... sober"*?

Sir Winston Churchill
named his horse after
his favourite brand of
champagne – Pol Roger.

True or false?

TRIVIA

ON

TAP

71

The term *'lager lout'* was
introduced by Esther Rantzen.

True or false?

Which nation are the greatest consumers of beer per head - drinking more than their consumption of milk, wine and soft drinks together?

a) Belgium
b) Germany
c) UK

If you were to sconce, where would you be, and what would you be doing?

a) *At Oxford University, partaking in a traditional drinking toast.*

b) *In Yorkshire, drinking very slowly.*

c) *In Cornwall, not standing your round.*

What is a Dog's Nose?

a) *A cocktail of beer and gin.*

b) *A traditional Kentish name for a hop-masher's pummel.*

c) *A weeping sore on the lips caused by drinking from dirty glasses.*

TRIVIA

ON

TAP

74

In the Far East pregnant

women and rheumatic miners

drink Benedictine as a tonic.

True or false?

In 1994 which vodka purveyor, owned by the British and managed by Americans, launched its first vodka produced in Russia since the Bolshevik Revolution in 1917?

Sir Walter Raleigh, potato discoverer and one-time beau of Elizabeth I, was fond of a drink: Which of the following events, if any, really took place?

a) At the Virginia Tavern in Wiltshire Raleigh was enjoying the fruits of his travels and having a puff on his pipe whilst supping his pint. All of a sudden an unwitting barmaid, afraid the great traveller was alight, doused him in beer to extinguish the flame.

b) Whilst locked in the Tower he had a small laboratory set up in his prison chambers in which he tried to distil a 'Great Cordiall'. Queen Anne of Denmark, a fan of Raleigh's, claimed the brew saved her life during a great illness. King James I was not so impressed, and Raleigh lost his head in 1628.

c) In 1595, on his way to Guyana in search of the mythical Eldorado, he stopped off on route at Cork to pick up a cask of Irish whiskey.

In the 1780's how
many gallons of gin
and brandy were
smuggled annually
into the UK?

TRIVIA
ON
TAP

78

Where did the American breweries Anheuser-Busch get the name Budweiser from?

a) Budweis was the name of the German brewery founder's first pet dog!

b) A German immigrant, Eberhard Anheuser, set up a brewery in St Louis Missouri in 1875, and launched the beer with the name that was synonymous in Czechoslovakia with the brews from the small town of Budweis.

c) The name is a bastardisation of the American word 'buddy' and Czech slang 'weis' meaning best.

In nineenth century America, what was 'nose paint'?

a) *Slang for liquor*

b) *The frothy head of beer*

c) *An ointment sold in mid-west towns, which was said to cure incorrigible drunkards by reacting with the smell of liquor to create a foul aroma.*

What is unique about the water used in beer production at Farson's Brewery in Malta?

a) *Farson's use rainwater collected in underground stores.*

b) *It is brought in from the Massif Central. (During a bad drought in 1976, they were forced to import bottled sparkling mineral water.)*

c) *It is collected from traditional Maltese cleansing pools, where the old and infirm bathe to benefit from the water's healing properties.*

Where does the expression 'Scot free' come from?

a) An English allusion to the supposed meanness of the Scots.

b) English urban pubs had to pay a tax known as a 'scot'. Any crafty pub-crawler who left the town for the country was lucky enough to find himself drinking 'scot free'.

c) Sir John Scot, who, after apprehending and killing a gang of brigands who terrorised inns on his manor in Kent, became a national hero, and was given a free drink at any inn he stopped at.

TRIVIA
ON
TAP

81

At one time it

was thought that

carrying the ashes

of the burnt livers

of frogs and hedgehogs

in a bag would cure

alcohol-induced

sexual impotence.

True or false?

In Australian drinking slang, how would one order a very small glass of beer?

a) *A butcher*

b) *A sheila's shandy*

c) *A Melbourne*

If there were two breweries in Edinburgh in 1996, how many were there in 1900?

a) 10

b) 14

c) 36

In 1944, under orders from Winston Churchill, the Board of Admirality converted two small mine-laying ships to 'amenity ships' which had on board cinemas, bars and breweries, for the British forces fighting against the Japanese. Distilled sea-water was used for brewing purposes.

True or false?

What is called 'a wailing of cats' in Germany, 'a wailing of kittens' in Poland and 'a pain in the roots of the hair' in Sweden?

a) *A cocktail of mint schnapps and pils*

b) *A hangover*

c) *The traditional reception for the drunken husband from his shrewish wife*

Whatis

a scuppernong?

a) A Maori name for an alcoholic
b) An Anglo Saxon drinking helmet
c) A type of white grape

In which East End pub was George

Cornell killed by The Krays?

a) The Auld Triangle

b) The Blind Beggar

c) The Dog and Bucket

TRIVIA
ON
TAP

86

SOLUTIONS

1.   Teetotal
2. c
     True
3.   b
4.   Because during the First World War the
     government forbade members of the
     general public from buying each other drinks.
5.   True
6.   b
7.   a) Artichoke
     b) Potato
     c) Strawberries
     d) Mushrooms
     e) Tea
     f) Coffee
8.   b – To prevent further disasters, she donated a
     sum of money to provide Hollands gin for
     eternity. It has since been the custom of the
     Company to offer their dinner guests a choice
     of brandy or Hollands gin with the time-
     honoured question, 'Do you dine with
     Alderman or Lady Cooper?'
9.   Drink becomes 'tiddly wink'
     Drunks: 'elephants trunks' becomes 'drunks'
     You are a drinker: 'on the booze' becomes
     'River Ouse'
10. Thomas Jefferson
11. b
     a) Courage
     b) Mackeson
     c) Harp
12. True
13. c. a and b are seventeenth century cures.
14. a
15. c
16. True
17. a

TRIVIA
ON
TAP

88

18. False
19. c
20. c
     b
21. b
22. a
23. The Victorian temperance campaign lobbied for shorter licensing hours. The landlords were in support of this campaign because far from cutting down on alcohol consumption, it simply cut down on overheads as drinkers quaffed equal amounts of booze – just quicker!
24. a
25. False – it is in fact the name given to a drink taken before breakfast.
     c
26. True
27. Macbeth
28. a
29. b
30. a
31. b
     You should pass the port, as the expression means you have been holding the bottle for too long!
32. a) champagne
    b) brown ale
    c) port
    d) vodka
33. Refusing to have a drink
34. c
35. 4
36. False
37. b
     False – it in fact means the opposite.
38. a
39. Lager
40. a
     Gin

41. a – A difficult and dangerous task on any ship, the reward was always a double shot of rum.

b – In the eighteenth century sailors consumed $^1/_2$ pint of rum as their daily rum ration and each $^1/_2$ pint was double the strength of today's commercial rum. In 1731 Admiral Vernon of the Royal Navy ordered that the rum was mixed to a ratio of one part rum to four parts water and dispensed in two draughts spread through the day. 'Grog', meaning rum and water, is said to derive from the nickname given to Admiral Vernon, who was known as 'Old Grog' because he wore a waterproof grosgrain cloak.

c – The sheets on a ship are the ropes controlling the sails. If they work themselves loose and flap in the wind, the control of the sail, and therefore the ship, is undoubtedly shakey.

42. Anthony Trollope

43. False
    a

44. True

45. c

46. c

47. c

48. a

49. Brandy
    c

50. b

51. c

52. b
    a

53. a

54. Abraham Lincoln

55. b

56. True

57. Newcastle. The Dog is an affectionate term for Newcastle Brown Ale, so called because taking the dog out for a walk was a well-used excuse by the henpecked husbands on the Tyne for a trip to the local pub.

TRIVIA
ON
TAP

90

58. False
    a

59. b

60. Tequila. The plant is known as Mezcal, and it is believed that the origins of the name Mexico come from the plant's name.

61. c
    Lloyd George 1915

62. c

63. a

64. He had him drowned in a barrel of his favourite tipple – malmsey wine.

65. True

66. El Lager

67. c
    c

68. True

69. Greta Garbo

70. True

71. False - it was in fact Tory MP John Patten.

72. b

73. a
    a

74. True

75. Smirnof

76. They all did!

77. 6 million: 2 million of brandy and 4 million of Geneva gin.

78. b

79. a
    a

80. b

81. True

82. a
    c

83. True

84. b

85. c
    b

TRIVIA
ON
TAP

LAGOON
BOOKS